SUDDEN DOG

SUDDEN

DOG

poems

MATTHEW PENNOCK

Alice James Books
FARMINGTON, MAINE

Alice James Books are published by Alice James Poetry Cooperative, Inc.,
an affiliate of the University of Maine at Farmington.

ALICE JAMES BOOKS
238 MAIN STREET
FARMINGTON, ME 04938
www.alicejamesbooks.org

Library of Congress Cataloging-in-Publication Data
Pennock, Matthew, 1981-
  Sudden dog : poems / by Matthew Pennock.
    p. cm.
  ISBN 978-1-882295-92-0 (alk. paper)
  I. Title.
  PS3616.E566S83 2012
  811'.6--dc23
                    2011049178

Alice James Books gratefully acknowledges support from individual donors, private foundations, the
University of Maine at Farmington and the National Endowment for the Arts. ❦

Image of Alice James by permission of the Houghton Library, Harvard University.
Call number: pf MS Am 1094, Box 3 (44d)

Cover design: Mary Austin Speaker

CONTENTS

ACKNOWLEDGMENTS

The author would like to thank the editors of these journals and periodicals in which the following poems first appeared, sometimes in different forms:

Denver Quarterly: "Lone White Bird on a Chimney"
LIT: "Apologia Ayatollah;" "Night Sweat"
Western Humanities Review: "Midnight on Montalto"
Spinning Jenny: "Beneath the Arctic Floe"
American Literary Review: "The Caged Children"
Guernica: A Journal of Art & Politics: "Big Money"
Love Among the Ruins: "Summary Wednesday;" "New World Constant;"
    "Theorem"
Mead Magazine: "Forgive the Hyena Its Crimes;" "Short Lease"
InDigest: "After Shooting the Texas Chupacabra;" "Goodbye, Downriver, My Love"

I thank Lucie Brock-Broido, Ricardo Maldonado, Erica Wright, Stephanie Anderson, Marilena Zackheos, Annabelle Yeeseul Yoo, and Julie and Jason McDougall for their advice, criticism, and encouragement. I would also like to thank everyone at Alice James Books, especially Carey Salerno, Laura McCullough, and Frank Giampietro. I would also like to express my love and gratitude to all my friends and family for their constant support. You all know who you are.

For my mother

FORGIVE THE HYENA ITS CRIMES

Each concussion, or possible concussion between car, or bus, or taxi,
      or pedestrian, or horse causes the eyes to cross and everyone triples
      as if three men wore the same suit at a wedding.

Perhaps, I expected too much from you, but I hoped an admission
      of weakness would make me appear vulnerable, thus more
      attractive, some injured riflebird, plumage still aquamarine
      and on display.

The sad-eyed hyenas rue the level of misunderstanding they face.
      They beg for someone to hear pain in those merciless
      cackles, to see remorse in the blood that spatters each muzzle.

They dream a caucus of zebra, buffalo, antelope, and gnu where
      they are lauded for their antagonism of the lion, and their efforts
      to keep the Serengeti sanitary. They awake, cold and frayed,
      in a world that takes hours to re-collect.

There are tears in blood, blood in drool. Head of dog, neck of horse, wrecked
      bone and quiet. Tears in drool, tears in tears, blood for blood. Leg
      of a cat rolled in cinder and mud.

At times, I lie on coastal rocks, long swaths of shale, blacker than
      the center of an eclipse, and I, entirely covered in long fur of ochre
      that troughs and crests in the gales of an approaching nor'easter.

This must be what heaven is like, line after line of furry beasts weaved
      around each other like skeins of yarn, then packed in saltwater,

each one eventually peeled off, cooked, then eaten the way the past
consumes more and more hours every day

until you blow open. Bloomed and emboldened, unburdened of seed or season.
    Say it again—blown open. Vulnerable to nothing because nothing's left,
    but a pure, harsh peal of your laughter shooting into the calm
    where it finally dissolves.

Beneath the Arctic Floe

This shrewd quotient,
spiraling and ridged like the fractal
geometry of a seahorse tail.

My new obsessions: electoral math,
Greenland sharks,
the doctrine of duck and cover.

Portrait of a symptom on the couch:

Sleeper, we are blind
and sometimes
eat our own.

The bed, too empty.

Sleeper, do not fear.
If you are buried with mortar and brick,
you have become too heavy.

Buildings do not collapse
due to fire or some
architect's mistake.

They grow tired simply—
our asking them to hold us.

ADDENDUM

The window, although free of fire, allows petty escape.
When it comes to payment (which it always does)
these pockets run deep, deeper than my thoughts,

which are sad, and on layaway.

It's not just me.

Everyone's tired. Everyone's
nerves are making them tussle.

The watershed proves its point
to shellfish: so much poison, so little time.

Algae blooms on the sunken iron of Chevys
beneath the Chesapeake Bay Bridge (another misguided
escape), sleeping in the phosphorescent
mood lighting of depth.

When you hear the news,
all the oxygen will wander from the room,
lips parted in a pantomime of something
resembling regret.

Just set the window frame aflame and leap
through like a circus poodle, leaving

you and the train to stop, intolerable squeal;
the soundtrack of leaving, horsehair bowed sharp,
and the platform plugs its ears.

I was going to call, but it was late.
You were probably sleeping.

Hephaestus Fashions an Adamantine Net

I want to see a bird. I want it dead,
dove-spill, nonchalant, and aubergine.

I have reasons for jar lids, their punched holes,
and the worm.

I want brawls and pistol-play
under Mama's warm chemise,
the *this* and more.

Spade and crypt, spoon-stone
split under the earth; a lever here,
six saw-toothed gears.

I was described as a gentleman once,
the heavy kiss an afterthought, and then

a sudden dog,
mange-splotches, the bareness
peaches undergo when bit,

muzzle the source
of sparseness and blight.

You got the Black Flux,
and I got crusaders scaling
my rampart again and again.

Summary Wednesday

Half the girls in this train car wear gold earrings, large and oval, bisected
    by their names in script. They are yours because you name them,
    your Lekenya, your Mirellie, your Yesenia.

Excessively ornate, almost illegible, like your grandmother's cramped
    handwriting in a Hallmark card with loopy golden cursive relaying
    every detail of the rest home in Orlando

where her former pastor now resides—the year of establishment,
    the founder's name, what the food is like, how once someone moves in,
    they have no plans of ever moving again.

Tomorrow, you settle on a plan for breakfast, you settle on banana. You are
    not hungry. It sits there on the desk still in peel, nervous for inevitable
    disrobing. Stare at Banana. You sit there. It is afraid.

POEM PHONED-IN FROM A NON-EXTRADITION COUNTRY

My friend built a fear bank.
I was his primary investor,

but now my temples are tight,
and charity is not for the tense.

The private globe can quickly tilt
into new seasons, like a fishbowl
on a rocking chair, water slapping
glass and arcing over the lip.

This water needs change anyway,
always too cold or too hot
and so much like a dream
until the day it is not a dream,

and that, Kitten, is what we call a reckoning.

Newton falters, leaving
only one motion, a violent plunge
toward the barren,

a burnt-black barn continually
collapsing and then rising again
in the smoke of another coup d'etat
where brothers hack
brothers by twilight.

Short Lease

Shelter: a place where nothing
never happens, manmade shade.

We become impenetrable,
encased in stone. Foolish,

just how a land bird on a boat is bad luck.
Small stowaway panics in the hold

where no fresh water stands unmarred
of sea spray or antifreeze.

It's the saddest thing, something wild
caught unaware in a strange place.

THE BLOODY EAGLE

Killing a king presents certain difficulties. Not locked in a tenebrous
   den (green-lit ancient rock still equals regal authority). In his own
   streets, he is lost, a ship unmoored and tossed in the aftermath
   of a tempest-struck harbor.

He must look sufficiently humiliated during de-crowning, preferably
   something involving nudity and tears. Let all of his former friends
   line up in plain sight, lips pulled fishhook—

An irritated window slams shut. Too late for elevated voices, too late
   for music, *but it's never too late for music* she says. The sound ricochets sharply
   down the stone gulf between yours and hers.

You are too dumb for refinement. Neither wine, nor roses, nor string quartet
   attach their mandibles to your thigh and leech. What's left of the host
   sustains no worm, buys no indulgence.

Take stock of the queen as she lies on the bed. She has two of each:
   arms, legs, eyes, breasts. All these together are eight, a perfectly
   adequate number, but add her sex and receive nine.

Nine, imbued with celestial power, nine muses, nine months, nine sacred
   Chinese rites, nine steps of Thor, Route Nine through Jersey, *nine
   ladies dancing*, nine players to a baseball team, Beethoven's Ninth,
   the number of Christ.

Nine times, foolish boy, you've let bygones be and held them up before
the summer becomes cinder and sweat. Such is your three-by-three,
such is the material that builds your citadel.

Watch her as she takes pleasure in a number. Her stomach, her hips,
her ass—and she says, *If only I could borrow your thoughts for just
one day*, but you cannot let this happen because of what it means
to not return.

Replacing a king presents more difficulties. The spectacle of execution alone
must suffice. If prone, he may be quarried, wealth transferred,
a caravan beset by bandits intent on burning the forest down.

Ribs separated from spine, one by one. The bone flexes just a little before
it snaps upward to take its place in a graceful row of arcs—
a frame for the lungs pulled out and over. You are a broken kite.

You are a cat-o'-nine-tails. You are the cruelest of birds waiting to take flight.

BIG MONEY

        suits me fine,
        I want to be loaded,

want God to cast me glances, treacherous
and elegant from beneath the brim
of his porkpie hat as if to say,

You played with the adversary
as a child, didn't you?

        I did, God, I did.
We played Steal the Bacon
and explored our unmentionables
behind the gazebo,

sat next to each other
in the School of Second Chances
where all the boys are cuntstruck,

        their grinding teeth, the industrial dirge
        of red whammies and other wrong answers,

and it's so boring,
listening to another person's dreams,
the fata morgana of natural
citizens who commission

army engineers to build
a bridge into the sky, across
which you can always
thumb a ride

to where Dorothy awaits,
blue cornflower riding up,
scissoring thighs,
and the tip of her finger
sheathed in tongue.

Scavenger's Daughter

You are condensed,
victim of charlatans
who ardently greet the unnatural.

Body in threes,
metal on metal on metal.
Only the sounds of waiting filter in:

A crick then a crack,
not the wheel, nor the rack,

rather the desire to rise,
wrestle possession and fail

more cities, more inventors
and their affairs of the craven
yet cunning maneuver.

Supplicant, sweetheart,
they call it justice, not swagger,
and it's always wrong
whatever you do.

it was determined to be a coyote.
How disappointing.

As is the day—

Miles away, hunters imitate ducks
in quiet wetlands,

    then a gunshot.

A group of birds squawk skyward.

The wind and the sun in their eyes,
    the reflection of the sun on water,
the lights like little suns
        make something happen.

They flicker like rebel gems,
golden rivulets of imperfect geometry.

The cocker retrieves and drops his quarry,

Expectant as an unlit candle,
a mausoleum of crowded tongues,

    he wants something Sicilian.

Many things emit notes of mourning:
saxophone, violin, dove, Sicilian.

What's left behind is—

What's left behind
      grows thinner every day.

That chupacabra loped in front of a cop car
      for miles.

Glancing back almost
if he knew he were being watched.

His moment—
Then a sound,
then the birds erupted skyward.

Self-Portrait as Fisherman

Tattoos,
not small, but sleeves. Perhaps something
with scales or something with thorns.

I say,
mothers everywhere
will not approve. And who
doesn't love mothers, the audience asks.

A cormorant explores the drain:
there's enough to eat down here, methinks,
enough to contend.

Upon return, the fisherman tugs the snare
and reaches down his bird's throat
to remove sweetfish.

In that period of forgiveness
between youth and competence,
clarity's the norm, understood
and assumed.

In that period, I was an asshole.

Metamorphosis in a Phone Booth

Last Night, empty wine bottles against the kitchen wall like patriots
        awaiting the justice of a junta death squad. Today,
        they have chosen to fall in the slow way that inspires fear
        among the frightened civilians.

Their dregs spatter the surrounding tile, dark red verging on purple
        mess as if someone killed a cat or codfish. A clamor, rhythmic
        metallic knocking of machinery in peril, or three people
        walking gingerly over the faces of the innocent dead.

It's not apples or oranges, but a cherry job to make your friends
        jealous. They'll quail in stews of marrow-envy when they
        see you emerge to fly counterclockwise around the equator
        until time seems to run backward,

just desserts for another idle hour. Up early and waiting for wedding
        bands, but no one ever calls. Take it as a lesson, a moment
        to reflect on choices: duties shirked, friendships overtaxed, days
        unplucked.

Consider what's required for your life to be a success: money, awards
        children surrounding a reclining bed with blue sheets
        in a white room suffused with electronics.

Imagine if your powers of deduction were unparalleled and you could
        see through walls. What crimes would you solve? What days
        would you take off for rest and recovery? The ratio is one grand
        larceny to seven Arabian Nights.

January, We Had No Hot Water

Blade-scraped bud
falling disrupted.

Loneliness is rest, nothing
to buckle across,

like the walk back over the parquet
when the prom queen declines.

I stepped into you, and nothing changed,
no eruption of brass,
no unseasonable birds taking flight.

Beneath the scaffolding
almost a four-year kiss,

but the long division unwraps
like tired gauze, one
suture, one split end.

Goodbye, Downriver, My Love

The midway's former tenants
must have offended the state

to suffer such eviction.
Pyramids of splintered clapboard,

and so much paper, wet and wadded.
The idols of my youth have all chosen

this season to die, one by one
they succumbed to bowel cancer

or accidental acute toxicity.
I can't blame them.

My blood wants only to desert
and waits for any opportunity.

Gone is the gypsy wagon, gone
the calliope, gone the fiberglass horse

with eyelashes to kill for. The carnival
is over and will never come again.

The remnants return to swamp as
new stalks of wild grass nod

out of time to the frenetic chorus
the night toads provide.

The Great Indian Rope Trick

A be-turbaned man squats, drum in hand, beating and beating three yards
   from a wicker basket. No defanged cobra. We know defanged cobras.
   We know they sway to music, to motion.

This is not magic but gravity. A thickly woven rope extends skyward. Light
   circles as hurricane-force winds in the tropics of deep space,

visible only to a powerful lens. Perhaps it's warm in the center, matter and
   meat distilled into molten cream like a fritter filled with seafood and corn
   moving backward across epochs

in which passenger pigeons reform and take to the air in flocks thick enough
   to blot out the sun. This is not magic but science. The rope stands stiff,
   Jacob's ladder rising ever further. It's a violation, a secret said to be lost.

The man waves his drum back and forth, its pounding growing faint, then
   unbearably loud. With each movement of his arm, the rope shifts from
   red to blue.

One man yells *it's magic*, another *it's only a trick*. The rustle of voices grows quiet as the man
   beckons to a young boy in the audience. He gestures: *Climb.*

The boy hesitates, then takes hold and ascends, eyes fixed skyward. He climbs
   hand over hand, until the soles of his feet disappear into cloud, never
   to be seen again.

NIGHT SWEAT

My pond water, my dead pool,
too much for towel and sheet.
Total immersion—
enough to change a man's mind

or matter.

I am any man you want me,
begging for the hook in the cheek,
the long pull to the surface.

Gut and stuff me, hang me on your wall
for the neighbors to admire.

I am a good fish, giving up once numb.

Apologia Ayatollah

Chest anvil, ball bearing heart,
stripped as a duplex
on the wrong side of town.

Already, so much
has been said
about so little,

my oboe solo to a sand viper.

I imagine your body
as pale as your hands.

What I want is hard to explain.
The deserted streets are Thursdays.
A conch shell is the sun.

Iron sleep attends,
wrecked and willing,
waking surprise of waking alive.

At the end of it all, I was quite
drunk on astonishment.

Three days a week, we sat still.
We sat shamed under the crushing weight:
love's sermon, a cut of light.

Theorem

The irregular room begs a lesson. A bald, bespectacled man could do
    wonders with the variation of angle; no turtle shell tesserae, all
    present save acute, so severely missed here.

That which makes me myself is no longer I.

I'm sure Pythagoras understands. In the number all is all, equations
    of the room may not be as such, but I am definitely squared.

The hardwood molding, reddish in hue and glossed with layers of wax,
    reveals the trapped remains of a thousand silent meals
    and the scavengers that subsisted on them.

Patterns emerge in biscuit and bread; a stray paper clip contorts the fringe of
    rug. The subdued rumble of hand against ear, softening the sound
    of a person eating, or warring houseflies,

but nothing is ever silence, it is heard again and again.

Patterns emerge in the lit windows of skyscrapers, they rise and fall
    as quarter notes in the staff of a minstrel's tune about the lighter
    side of the whip and its reason.

I awake; I say get dressed. The hardwood gives way to tile, to stair,
    to threshold, to credulity, to stair, to tile, to concrete. No apt
    metaphors, no numbers, no patterns, only the weather and how
    it will treat us today.

Yesterday afternoon, the stock exchange stumbled again and be-suited men seem downtrodden, but why should I care? This is how you string a noose; this is how you set up a joke; this is how you give up.

II

DAYS OF ABANDONMENT

Another five-dog night
heaving fur,
breath trapped and rank, damp fingers running.

So many days wasted diving, long descent
                        and a few moments to sift mud,

bivalve and hinge—solid seems to disperse,
                                        been living awhile.

Marilena calls *Good Boy* enough
time put in on those knees.

You can never fill that bucket,
or get back on—
                        so try again.

A farrow in rind and bone
at ceramic works where the kiln
lies beyond repair.
                        The sad pottery
slowly caves like the hardest word
when you don't believe

and must say it over and over.

———

In the style of winter,
                    a stiff reality spilling gray

on wool accoutrements.

I chose elusive, inconsistent
with the occasional flash of wit.

Marilena is hydrogen,

and the eyes of all determined walkers
                              are penitent;
the wind content
to roll Chinese food menus
until someone looks up

                    and suffers its dry retort.
The tears, involuntary, but passersby
still suspect a death.

Still, we look up
as one who awakens on his back,
                    knows the day is long,
and asks questions of the ceiling,

                         which chips away
to expose a patch of concrete
in the shape of an unmistakable country,

the setting of our poor postmodern epic
with only the occasional
stab of envy

felt by assassins who never actually
fall on their swords.

———————

The fog roiled under streetlamps,
                        and, Marilena,
I was in my whisky happiness
while talking to you of epics

and how to properly blanch tomatoes,
which were once thought poisonous
                        like adder,
        which as long as I hold
you beneath my tongue,

        I have no reason
        to fear because

snakebite puts me in the mood,

and the judge
who decides our sentence
will dangle modifiers

and help the blind ensure
a prosperous life

        because the braver boys
                who go to war
come home in pieces,
and ready for supper.

———

Awoke in a mess of my own making
                              and swore
I felt her move
until five years flash flooded the alley

and cracked all the stained glass
of another unholy Sunday.

                              Snow flirted for weeks,
finally kept its date last night,
but left after a few hours,
all the trains delayed.

Everyone has excuses
in the amethyst hour when soon becomes
                              too late.

Marilena thistle blooms
in toxic wine   o those arabesques
cannot be followed,

so foolish, not myself,
trembling in wait at the front door,
                      while a star-throated locust
thieved the window.

I've already made arrangements:

I will vacation somewhere far,
where newlyweds
carefully groom each other
in the moonlight.

―――――

Pressed to wound,
inflating,
      liquid defying gravity solidifies,

an orb turning end over end,
           andante.

A cosmic lunch, or ball of girl in red nightgown,

too short, the way a length of rope
can stretch from the gallows only so far
        if it's to achieve the desired effect.

Marilena as martyr, red and white,
        Marilena as gauze.

Young boys beneath
hoplons take the owlet
for protection as long
as it covers the next man,   and so on.

It's the momentum you must rely on,

you can waste years that way—

Swelling masses above the sacrum,
                and the doctors want to drain,
but darling,

       doctors don't know anything.
They just test and test.

Must be the plague—

        brought on by evil thoughts
and more red meat.

When Marilena plays a witch,
she raises the dead and forms an
army to storm Camelot

        or to torture her cat
who stalks the exposed flesh that affronts him.

           and when her danger nears,
the light dims enough to make
pasting the dictionary
        impossible,
the practice of poets who know
a rhinoceros is not a rhinoceros,
but can't see the spinning halogen
          of the bridge tower

split the mist tonight.

———————

Want of modesty, want of exuberance,
                    but the gaff cutter sails untouched
from the harbor,

the water weevil abandons rice
because this rare, fat, pink moon over the factories
of the meadowlands

began with the blood of Medusa:
                                        first seaweed
then hardened as concrete and shale

which belies
the building in which I stand.

Not really sure how I got here,
                    but there lay two wet feathers,

pigeon-shed, pasted to pavement.
                              I want to lick them,
to know their taste then lose it,

the way Marilena loses her hue
when her bones build a palace
                    reflecting the intent of visitors

who harm children,
or make the endless day longer
with the dark cursive of the otherwise unruly.

———

      Burn stone, three hundred
and ninety-two degrees and rising—

            black colophony
leaching into linseed oil.

Varnish the feather, the tress.
Forgive Marilena, for her smell, for the weakness
                      it inspires,

want of scent litters
the night with dyspepsia
             and wand'rings of lung—

we will never win,
and we will never forget the damage we cause,

but if there is such a thing as luck,
              perhaps we will be forgiven.

Breathing seemed
the right thing to do, even
             if it was smoke,
or dank, sweat-thick air

of a room that is too small for two,
where I envied everyone
           with the ability to sleep easy.

———————

Something's going to happen soon, she says,

the tests all inconclusive,
           California left without almonds.

      We take agriculture for granted,
years and years of cultivation,

                drought resistant, high yield
and still nothing here to eat.

Abnormal warmth
and the trees all fooled.
The drones have stormed out over stolen honey.

      I understand their point,
all that space and nothing
              of value to fill it.

Consider the pomegranate with its difficulties,
no flesh to savor, no work worthwhile.

The petals are the exact color
I painted them,
            beckoning anything
to come and drain the orchard's surplus nectar.

A man swaddled in mesh
fills the glade with smoke.

The hives empty, steadfast,
wait for a queen who never comes.

———————

Cure me of dropsy,
liquid pooling in the lesser regions
of ankle and shin,

a lake
in which Marilena waited,
clutching the triple-encrusted hilt.

Let's make it a gift,
                        just to be rid of it,

pawn it off on the next cat
that feigns interest

before he turns his back to find a better corner to nap.

Jacinth in its clearest form,
                masquerades diamond
on all continents hospitable to magpies.

You brilliant little fake,
we've so few places in common—

                Berlin, Nicosia,
we like our cities with walls to split them.

And what of love?
Its little turret for the watch,

necessary as eating
even if the jaw is wired,
or persistently cankered,

I have this to thank:
the woman who promised to feed me
when it becomes impossible to do so of my own accord.

I dreamt a Chinese funeral in the first century:
corpse armored in green,

                    another life promised,
but it won't be here,

and that's good enough.

On this side of the wall,
the rooms musty with displaced earth,
underground chamber to underground chamber

filled with ceramic circuses
                    and dead courtesans.

The mahjong circle committed to north wind,
which never strips the traveler until
                                    the sun has its say.

Your mouth, a cadaver
where I placed a stone as large as a billiard ball
cleft in half; thumb-top moon sits on the tongue.

Rainmaker,
so much is told by the teeth
and what path they have chosen.

We come back to life again and again, Marilena.

Oblivion is too heavy,
                    too much vacation
for a want such as ours that fuels

a temple and a terracotta army
beneath the sand.

When they unearth us,
they'll have hell to pay.

———————

The atmosphere rent, unstuffed, someone
who is unspeaking   speaks

                        to the only bright window
of a red brick apartment complex
on the corner of two poorly lit streets
in central Virginia.

It's a relief,
        the night smell
of bluegrass and hydrangea, quivering
with the movements of the creatures they house,
absorbed with collection.

Marilena saw a groundhog here for the first time
and was perplexed
                by its complacency.

Unlike those city rats, brazen
but sly,   never far
from a bolt-hole.

In other times,
behind their venetian blinds,
the young anticipate something untried

and eye each other uncomfortably
across the room.

———————

Marilena born on a jet in Cypriot Airspace,
      hence her divided heart.

I wonder, darling,
if they passed each other
when they crossed the Green Line.

Did they look up,
    make eye contact?
Did they move into each other's houses
or burn them to the ground?

     The mourners sit unwashed
and rattle strings of jet,
tangled and worn-out,

like mouflon that roam abandoned towns,
chewing in that slow way.

Jet, the stone of flappers and Victorians alike,
of which Marilena is both

because she loves the idea of sex
with anyone she does not love,

yet can never bother to decide,
      and usually stays home.

But what good are decisions, I say;
they always end something:

a wall that no one bothers to climb,
trimmed with trip wires
     and men on high alert.

The other side is
just not that alluring anymore.

The ceiling's irregular hexagon,
trimmed with postcards, bad vision
                    of blurry basilicas and exposed teeth.

Conquerors always rename churches,
conical spires, draped
with crescents and stars,

                    through a spyglass, looking north,
where kings were made,

a slice of envy, a slice of concern,
sandstone and jasmine enclosed
in venetian walls.

Marilena reads only for mistakes,

and that's how I learned a lesson
                    about where to place my heart.

On the last day of every month,
some sort of god wears blue

and loses any hope of fidelity
among the coastal ruins of ecru and flax,

                    where she sleeps with an answer,
only to awake and discover its escape.
It went something like this:
Home is never home,
It has too many people to please,
        too many who want you to stay.

      Leave us assaulted
between crescendo and cross.

Marilena, those Russians turned Frederick the Great
east to face them.

      Finger of light bisecting the bed, my face;
I found it hard to sleep, but

we do things because they are hard.

On cold pavement, hypothermic,
                             unconscious
under the lindens,

where serrated leaves
like trilobites litter—
          a basalt ruin offering its treasures

               the way a disappointment
of lovers rue their scarred hearts under
an embarrassment of stars.

Nine-hundred years we have had the compass,
                      and still
          I have trouble with direction.

Iron struck by lightning and magnetized
      is lodestone,
magic to the ancients and the titans of industry
who choose their sides by reputation
and leave us in the field, ashamed.

———

Five years spent static, massaging sternum,

massaging throat

for an irregular yesterday.

This city of bridges, therefore,

city of promise, city of lies.

Predawn explosions

stare at fire trucks with no reward,

and hooded men seem important

with places to go.

I am game as well and have hidden

nothing beneath

my tongue.

Marilena awoke

to find her clothes

in the refrigerator,

but this we cannot hold against her she explains.

When one returns to something,

it's always stressful;

bourbon has done it to me again, this time

from a coffee mug,

ripe with hunger,

and troublesome light

left over as moon-rust

in parallel lines.

I promised myself I wouldn't steal,

I promised myself.

It's about need, I guess.

                    We lay close, not touching.

If it were a still life

it would be Desolate Tuesday.

———————

I had a cough that adored an ambush,
               and you weren't picking up your phone.

I'm not the genius I thought I was, or even
avant-garde,
                         but I'd like to think
I'm good company.

               It's certainly uneven,
the amount of thought I put into livestock,
fenced and bleating,
one following the other

               until they're without the other.
Why, Marilena, do they keep walking

       when walking seems the hardest thing to do?

I keep staring down the alley
and calling again.
                         A crackle of static,
an unintelligible voice bleeds through
a megaphone and bounces
from tenement to tenement.

The rain is not hard,
                 but it will cover us all.

Marilena, I'm tired, maybe tomorrow
the world will get right,

                         maybe tomorrow,
I'll awake and breathe unencumbered,

new air, saturated and green.
Spring again.

––––––––

Every morning requires
                 a different belt notch—

growing bolder with weight
as how a balding man reaches for the maidservant's hem,
       first hesitant   then a fistful of lace.

             I grew a mustache,
à la madcap equestrian,
sick with perfume of magazines,
and hid matches in a beer can.

Marilena of the black
and pink sweatpants,
do salamanders spit?

Do months pass easier
             when names slip away?

The conclusion is one of my poor character,
which I deserve, which is longer
than I expected to wait.

           Another coldest day of the year,
water boiling ruby and the poison all gone.

———————

Something foreign to be drawn,
eye-sting, cuts a lash
for wishing.

          Marilena fell into a trance,
dowsing rods cross,
and the end table dances.

The moment was false,
          but sincere in context,

the way funnel-webs trek for a mate
and rear like horses
when threatened,

like royalty, darling,
          always paranoid, always looking
for a crown of thorns
to wear with bravado.

If I had not just left it at that,
but asked for one more night
with all the things

for which I walked miles, lost and then just let go;
          despicable, really.

          At that moment,
I wish I had said something.

III

White Heat

Doggish, nose pressed to glass, occasionally
wiping away the fog of my own damp breath,
and I'm not tired,

just drunk and considering self-immolation
like Quang Duc who sat so peacefully in flame.

The industry stretches on. A row of metal globes
like the one Cagney stood atop before he exploded.

When did I start imagining these scenes in color?

There's always work waiting at the end of the line,
a month's worth of dishes, stacked and breeding,

two bottles of Drano to unclog the shower,
two bottles until I'm free from the plague of girl hair.

The bridge marks the Pennsylvania border.
In profile, red and green lights, flashing

between St. Andrew's steel crosses. Another mile
traveled, and it seems so much of my life consists

of waiting for the other shoe to drop, but I will not,
I will not die in Delaware tonight.

TRY NOT TO DISTURB THE EELS

On the docks, men finger their waistbands for flesh or metal and stare hard.
    They wait for you to hoist yourself onto the muddy bank.

For a little while, you may feel unsafe but undeterred. Hands pinned beneath shoulders,
    knees sliding in wet earth, you are vulnerable.

You shouldn't walk alone at night beneath the bridge, to the city limits. Out of town,
    the service road narrows as the grasses venture farther and farther
    into the asphalt isthmus.

Sure, the air is perfect and the view across the river is beautiful. The city lights
    suspended like a fete of pixies frozen between ages of myth, but are they
    worth it?

I have forgotten what you know, what it is to look into a man's eyes and know
    he means you harm. To see his shoulder cocked, his arm jerk, his fingers curl
    around each other, the sudden thrash.

Do not be afraid. You must go back to the river. You must remove your shoes,
    your pants, your shirt.

They are down there, deep in the mud, writing an alphabet of S's in the bottom.
    Splash loudly. They are down there. They will squirm. They will sink
    their pencil-tip teeth into your calf, but step hard, they will congregate.

No Coyote, No Artist

Pile of felt, garden gloves,
shepherd's crook,

the day is apolitical,
a day for sleeping at the foot of a tree.
Pillow-root,
wander, sheep, wander.

If ever there were a time for epiphanies,
it would be right now.
It would happen right now

in the form of one hundred bronze catfish
suspended above a pool,

gills leaking
a deluge that could save
a small Wyoming town
from a brush fire.

But there is a suspicious absence,
no fire alarms, no kickbacks,

only a map of Atlantis
after its sinking,
frozen waves, incisor sharp and wicked.

Everything here belongs outdoors.

I steal a hat and stroll into the West Garden.

WELL-WISHING THE ONES WHO NEVER ARRIVE

You are one who wants patience.
The sort it takes to build a roux,
consistent stir, long and slow
until the color becomes tarnished penny

that knows torrential late afternoons
of late summer will soon arrive to ruin this road,
which is not a road,

but a torn sheet of navy blue jersey,
which is not a sheet, but the starless evening
of another forgotten Friday
on the brink of total saturation.

Here, it is monkey see, monkey do.
It is run or be run over.

You are a broken puppet cavorting in barbed wire,
as strangely dignified as an albino peacock
in a churchyard, head tilted to improve reception
of the beggar hum, a call for alms

mouthed in barely audible tones,
by those who joined the line too late,
but wait just the same.

Scarecrow, I'll Miss You Most of All

Heartland's beating so fast, Darlings,
it may just pop
out of the amber waves of grain.

We found the children in the garden again,
wild-eyed, digging for roots.

Where are your parents, little ones?

Vacant gaze and open sore,
they're in the basement stirring iodine

and battery's sting,
dash of lye and owlet wing
for a charm of powerful trouble,

hellbroth boil and bubble.

Why must you pester us?

A wholesome tongue is a tree of life.
If you are quiet, the Lord will provide.

Front yards littered with steel pots crusted
with crystals like little yellow stained teeth,
and the West Coast pharmacy business is booming.

They can't keep the shelves stocked.
Take your medicine, little ones, and don't cry.

It's only America.

We watch it unravel like a fourth act without direction,
the actors blunder through,

and you are there and you are there and you!

Just stop it.

Stop flirting with the thought of who will come
if you jump, who will clean this twister's mess.

Remember, my darlings, not to strain yourselves
remember there is an old Spanish proverb: *It is not
the burden, but the overburden that kills the beast.*

If you only had a brain, you'd know you're the straw that breaks.

INTERIOR DECORATING

Red seems the dominant color,
but that may have something to do
with the excess oxygen in the room.
Argyle and twisted stalk,

so much made of it glad
for the conjuring: wheat, barley, rye—
the conversation dies as we stare
at opposite walls. No one falls.

No one wishes for a little brother
to paint over their contribution.
One movement begs a fix, another a stitch.
We lay down, unsure of our limbs bound

like cleavers in sheaths of cotton. Like to like,
unsure whether to attract or repel.
We are protected, you say, *from cold.*
After all, it's the body that dies so well.

Oh, but it's friction and the fire it makes.
In another country, large men
leave their huts before dawn
and measure wealth in terms of skull.

When it rains, they sink to their knees
in mud to thank the season for its bounty.
And you say, *This is how you see a room as more
than a room.* Lord, give us peace. Give plenty.

EVENTS SUBSEQUENT TO AN ADMITTED WRONG

The last whim of a Mayan god in exile leads
to a sudden reversal of current,

the dark cerulean
switches back and the trawlers, barges,
and skiffs broker a new deal.

Ore returns to strip mine, steel to smelt.
A saraband to the western shore
of when something mattered.

Tonight old men drink deep
and celebrate their sons for the last time.

A sudden arrival in another place,
the herald of a year better than the last,
or the wet blessing of familiar lips.

It's not complex, the hope of modern
architecture, its height and its daredevil
wire on which beautiful men lie.

From the rooftop, we stood immersed
in the torch-red of a warning light,

the castle tops of synagogues below,
squares of Morse code repeating
the letter O, a forgotten plea for rescue

that becomes your mother's intentions crushed
into an envelope of cash
pressed into your palm at the airport.

LONE WHITE BIRD ON A CHIMNEY

So be candid, be kind,
and stand the pigeon's roost

outside the window, though plumage
may constitute a skull.

Feather, feather,
we look good together,
restless in bed,
perched atop my head.

Forgive the flesh as awkward,
new tufts of hair,
penchant to flag into layers.

Those who are faithful,
know better hours arranging
peeled skin and lost strands

into dead languages
where everything is easy.

HYDROTHERAPY

Water in its purest form remains blue, a slight tint, but blue nonetheless.
    Not some added chemical, not the reflection of sky. Sixty
    percent of our bodies (give or take a few points), therefore, we are not
    honey, peach, or mocha, burnt umber, taupe, or blush.

For example, I am blue today. Not to say I am sad, but actually wearing
    all blue. It wasn't on purpose. I didn't wake up this
    morning and come to a firm decision about what to wear. It's just
    that these past two weeks monochrome has become an occurrence,
    both frequent and odd.

Even in the depths of your heart's strange aquifer, where the bedrock teems
    with translucent prawns, you can trust in the spectrum and where on it we fall,
    though it may seem too dark to tell.

In the Shadow of the Whale

So much for brotherhood—outside throngs of hairy people rustle in cold
      weather regalia and flood the surrounding boutiques, mouths
      open like farmed catfish.

This town remains too small, and we grow sadder for it. I'm sure
      even in this state, your fluke could swim, politely, but as it stands
      we will abide this current's arrangement a little longer;

I stare into the tunnel of your empty ribcage, an unfinished canal,
      an impossible beginning, that first gulp of air, the first shrill
      cry that falls on new ears.

It is better inside, white walls, wood floor— quiet as Baja's winter
      coast, yet I'm only a sack of blood and fat and bone moving
      from side to side, then back again, full of angry politic and cash
      poorly spent.

The sky opens and the meanest season has its way with the ground,
      raises it inches and postures a threat to all of us who dwell
      warm-blooded and overtaxed in this six horse town. It seems
      everything dies, but me.

I survive to go outside and eat and drink and work and eat again and curse
      and spit and drink until I'm a stupid fish and sleep and wake
      and work and sleep again, while something far better than me
      cruises the winter coast and disappears.

I swim as far as my arms will take me, leaving nothing for the return
  to shore. When you can't see land, when direction's lost, the only thing
  left is swimming in icy waters.

The trick is to sink all the boats that occasionally use sonar. Punch
  holes in their hulls with your smiling mug, the ironic smirk
  that hides a row of curved railroad spikes.

The Orcas know this. They believe in you. Pods traveling for miles
  in pursuit of seal, to the Arctic Circle and back. They dismiss
  our unnaturally blue swimming pools.

the way you detest the line in the post office and the unfriendly
  workers that decide whether your package will ever reach
  its destination, or remain lost on a concrete floor, harboring things
  long-spoiled or past time-sensitive.

We lament your purgatorial delivery status, the way a man thinks
  about breakfast and whether or not he will have it. Either way
  it doesn't matter except for mood,

and mood is overrated. The day still begins and the cars move in waves
  down the boulevard, first far between, then in a quick and inconstant
  roar.

I've forgotten many things, and I'm not sure I'll remember them all when
        the time comes: the morning and its creaks, the wooden floor,
        the sound of bone colliding with bone, and fluid flooding the cracks.
        Some country tune about love loss makes worse the gray light
        about the window.

The shower shrieks into action, and you stand naked under its product.
        Aware of only two things: water and its sound off the ceramic
        like radio static.

Work beckons once again, not some siren song, but rather an atonal
        rattle in the eaves that must be investigated before we can sleep
        in peace. They say you live longer if you have something to finish,
        I don't know—

I think we forget how to stop swimming—through avenues, through banks,
        through offices, through bedrooms, through Brooklyn trains.
        Movement begetting movement,

following red traffic lights or red signs in donut shops that read "Fresh
        out of the oven," ceasing to believe in anything but the seal
        and its bright meat forming roses between the waves.

Latitude remains a simple set of lines unheeded in the winter sea. There is
        only the swim, the hunt, and the return south. Always wanting
        South until we finally reach a shore on which to crash, rolling
        once over on the sand.

On Not Having a Self-Cleaning Oven

Four-year-sediment submits, at least
the majority, to Brillo.

Some prayer never taught, never tried,
but necessary. Stubborn mahogany streaks

immune to the incessant back and forth
of bicep and wrist. So many meals

merged into grit: pork fat, summer
squash, provolone. The abdomen bent tight

over the door and aching. Ash,
metal, and stone coalesce to make soap

as Olmec women wash clothes in the aftermath
of sacrifice. Piles of linen range

from raw umber to black. When the job
is done, supper is taken cold, over the sink.

THE QUEER OCCURRENCE OF MATTHEW PENNOCK AND THE GARGANTUAN MOTH

But first, at work there was a moth.
Loping flight, low pitch wave,
the size of a finch or small robin.

Customers screamed and ducked.
I pursued and cornered.

Slow turn, a charge,
diamond-grid ellipses
bluish gray and wild,

I looked the beast dead in the eye,

caught it mid-flight in my hands,
and ran to the balcony to release it
because, like all just conquerors,
I am merciful,

but I must have clipped a wing
because it descended to the sidewalk
in a flat spin.

Men approach the prospect of impotence
with a desperation dwindling
into the habitual.

I'm sorry, amateur butterfly.
I shouldn't have plucked you from the atmosphere,
shouldn't have stolen you like the hard kiss

Mary gave me at her front door,
the one with our entire bodies.
And when it ended, I swear I tasted blood.

ARCHAEOLOGISTS

Drawn as a young man to maps and manifestos, pamphlets designed
    to destroy the known world and replace it with a numinous sphere
    of concentric circles of blue light like a cartoon atom, I decided to dig.

With each plunge of the shovel and the ensuing heave, deeper and deeper we go.
    In our yearned for childhoods, forgotten uncles told us if we kept at it, if we
    remained committed and not susceptible to the distractions of the bumblebee,

we could pierce the surface of the other side and emerge in some
    undiscovered pleasure dome of Shangri-La where animals speak
    philosophy in radio plays, wise men wear beards of one hundred meters,
    and the dead are not dead, but made fire in the night.

It is always there under a mile of sand, the pyramid's tip over-tripped.
    Swept away in circles, again and again, dig a little deeper, you'll find it.
    More structure is all we need. More La Scala, more Hoover Dam.

SYSTEMS OF CHANCE

It comes down to a question of order:
car engulfed in flames; man walks out of car.
After awhile, circumference
doesn't matter, neither does height.
Your heart can't bear the fall
and gives up.

Maybe it's mercy.
Your loss, a small fraction,
one in scores
like alcoves of bird vertebrae,
or midafternoon, the rooms
deserted, thick.

This weather could steal
your romance, so everyone's
taking a risk. Bee sting or brick,
each carry delight
in their systems of chance.

I dislike it when strangers walk too close,
or if they're walking a good distance ahead.
I like mint, lists, and the press of bruises.

The strategy for making everything worthwhile
shifts like an awkward dancer bent
on seduction,

pounding the floor and flailing
as thunder claps so hard it sets off
all the car alarms on the street.

THE HEAD OF JOAQUIN MURIETA

Every circus side, every carnival has a whiskey jar
of wood liquor and those half-closed eyes
rolled up white,

on display between the Amazing
Turtle Boy and the Golden Snake of India.

Years after the rangers rode to town
with their grisly prize,
miners still found their camps ransacked
in his name.

They put his head on display,
and he lined up with the rest
and laid down his dollar,
stared, smirking, into his own lipless O.

While hundreds of forgeries
jostle cross-country in colorful wagons,
if one should fall, just replace it;
as the lawmen say one Mexican head
is as good as another.

It takes a real man to be a thief.
Sometimes, it takes a real man to be a liar.

MIDNIGHT ON MONTALTO

And always the slow ticking
of taillights on the highway to the west,

rusty second hand marking the miles
to a vanishing point cut into the Blue Ridge crest,

all the lights combining in a bluish white half-moon fading
up into space as distance fades around a sphere,

and then in a sudden divide, hairpin-sharp,
an expanse of stars,

one for everyone alive and then more,
varying degrees of intensity, so many

fireflies, trapped and wriggling
on the flypaper sky.

THEORETICAL PHYSICS

The universe began with no bang, but simply unwound, grew taut,
and I can try to rise, but when I collapse again

it is due to the mercy of ruthlessness and gravity.
Call it dancing. Call it two hundred thousand tons of metal and concrete

disappearing into ground. Call it the mujahideen lament
twisting the trouble clef. Call it—

answers become the size of spoons disclosed to the feeding blind,
and the brilliant insomniacs measure questions with exponential math.

As they stare at the rubble, men gather, hands pocketed, yellow hard hats
clustering like loose electrons. One steps into the floodlights.

We are connected, he says, *in the invisible* and *the invisible.*
There are more dimensions, seven, maybe, eight. You'll need us.
          We cut steel.

New World Constant

When I leave my room, does it still exist as mine, or does it require presence
        to infuse ownership? Do my bedclothes rise and fall in my absence
        as if covering an invisible sleeper, some other me

who travels without losing parts of himself? Tiny seeds floating through cracked walls
        fall in some other life and grow like rumors of infidelity.

Cut to a scene of a spoon on top of a drain, hot water running over until
        whatever was stuck, whether hardened cheese or chocolate, begins
        to lengthen and break, swept into the little Charybdis of the sink.

They begin their journey into the unkown plumbing, precious Columbuses,
        ballsy, but evil. The Arawaks await.

We're all waiting for something, Charlie Brown. The Great Pumpkin visits
        only the sincerest of patches, and we have not a shred of hypocrisy here.

The lights all out, the demons drunk on barley wine, tomorrow we will begin
        again, and this time I promise I won't leave you in bed with a stranger.
        His breath an irregular rasp, wet on your shoulder.

In the meantime we can explore the forest, catalogue and collect: Dutchman's
        throat, sailor thistle, snakethrush, bell bonnet, King James's blue thorn,
        spade-headed sharkweed— I can name a thousand, and not a one
        needs to be real.

The Caged Children

It was unsafe to have them roaming
about at night. Don't mourn their fates.

They were not born to inherit.
One of them would eat anything:

fertilizer, fistful of marbles, a nine-volt battery.
Another set a skirt hem aflame, and a small

girl had to be rolled on the grass until only
steam lifted off her. They need constant

supervision. They need structure—
that's why we put them to work

in the garden. We teach them to grow
things. We teach them the simple comfort

of a world with four walls close by,
the solid reliance on iron and wood.

It is all right. The police were also baffled.
Believe these children lucky; they know

what we cannot, the coffin comfort.
Nothing gets in. Nothing gets out.

Notes on Sub-Zero Survival

Teach the un-housebroken pets
they are not less than,

but rather some strange admonition
to the way things ought to be.

You should have read the signal,
the important farce that delves deeply

into the separation of man from his parts,
this simulacrum of what constitutes a life

in a world that deals strictly
in numbers, which, most often, seems

hyperbolic, or cold, but how we live.
The snow falling wet, it sticks

to all but the area we tread, or where exhaust
holds sway over an ellipse of tar, and we know

our joy will be only as fleeting
as the quiet world of bryophytes,

another lichen that survives Antarctic wind,
another moss on the south side of an oak

wondering why everyone walks the wrong way.
The travelers stop before nightfall

and build a shelter from litter and snow.
As they close in on one another for warmth,

the animals arrive to hunt, dreaming
of making beds in the rain. They move

feverish and slow as drunken stems lean
toward a vision of some other easy living.

BOOK BENEFACTORS

Alice James Books and Matthew Pennock would like to thank the
following individuals who generously contributed toward the publication
of *Sudden Dog*:

Book Benefactors

Anonymous
Anonymous
John & Kathy Harden
Davin Rosborough & Eric Hupe
Jason & Julie McDougall

Additional Contributors

Thomas Bell
Ricardo Maldonado
Michael & Cynthia Savage

For more information about AJB's book benefactor program, contact us via
phone or email, or visit us at www.alicejamesbooks.org to see a list
of forthcoming titles.

RECENT TITLES FROM ALICE JAMES BOOKS

Western Practice, Stephen Motika
me and Nina, Monica Hand
Hagar Before the Occupation | Hagar After the Occupation, Amal al-Jubouri
Pier, Janine Oshiro
Heart First into the Forest, Stacy Gnall
This Strange Land, Shara McCallum
lie down too, Lesle Lewis
Panic, Laura McCullough
Milk Dress, Nicole Cooley
Parable of Hide and Seek, Chad Sweeney
Shahid Reads His Own Palm, Reginald Dwayne Betts
How to Catch a Falling Knife, Daniel Johnson
Phantom Noise, Brian Turner
Father Dirt, Mihaela Moscaliuc
Pageant, Joanna Fuhrman
The Bitter Withy, Donald Revell
Winter Tenor, Kevin Goodan
Slamming Open the Door, Kathleen Sheeder Bonanno
Rough Cradle, Betsy Sholl
Shelter, Carey Salerno
The Next Country, Idra Novey
Begin Anywhere, Frank Giampietro
The Usable Field, Jane Mead
King Baby, Lia Purpura
The Temple Gate Called Beautiful, David Kirby
Door to a Noisy Room, Peter Waldor
Beloved Idea, Ann Killough
The World in Place of Itself, Bill Rasmovicz
Equivocal, Julie Carr
A Thief of Strings, Donald Revell
Take What You Want, Henrietta Goodman
The Glass Age, Cole Swensen
The Case Against Happiness, Jean-Paul Pecqueur
Ruin, Cynthia Cruz
Forth A Raven, Christina Davis

Alice James Books has been publishing poetry since 1973 and remains one of the few presses in the country that is run collectively. The cooperative selects manuscripts for publication primarily through regional and national annual competitions. Authors who win a Kinereth Gensler Award become active members of the cooperative board and participate in the editorial decisions of the press. The press, which historically has placed an emphasis on publishing women poets, was named for Alice James, sister of William and Henry, whose fine journal and gift for writing went unrecognized during her lifetime.

TYPESET AND DESIGNED BY MARY AUSTIN SPEAKER

Printed by Thomson-Shore
on 30% postconsumer recycled paper
processed chlorine-free